A KALEIDOSC

D. J. Rendle

In Loving Memory of ALL, the Golden Hearted People, in my past, (and Maiden Aunt Fanny) and *for:—* Joy and Peace.

ARTHUR H. STOCKWELL LTD.
Elms Court   Ilfracombe   Devon
Established 1898

© D. J. Rendle, 1997
First published in Great Britain, 1997
All rights reserved.
No part of this publication may be reproduced
or transmitted in any form or by any means,
electronic or mechanical, including photocopy,
recording, or any information storage and
retrieval system, without permission
in writing from the copyright holder.

British Library Cataloguing-in-Publication Data.
A catalogue record for this book is available
from the British Library.

ISBN 0 7223 2919-9

Printed in Great Britain by
Arthur H. Stockwell Ltd.
Elms Court   Ilfracombe
Devon

CONTENTS

Blackpool — 1994	5
An Ode to Grandad	6
Giggles	7
The Joy of a Job	8
Hopes	9
1994 — *D-Day* and *Remembrance* — 50 Years On	10
Blood Sportsmen!	12
In Support of Teddy Bears	14
To All *Would-Be* Valentines — (1994)	15
Ilfracombe — of the 50s	16
Love's Hopes — From a Wheelchair	17
For the Sake, of a Chip!	18
Praise and Care for Our Elderly and Veterans — ('95)	19
Burnt Toast!	20
Non-Sence! — At *The Sales*	21
A Little "Hope" Filled Pleasure	22
Sort Out Priorities — First!	23
United — The Whole Journey Through!	24
Some Limericks of Fun!	25
Football!	26
An Ode to the Clowns!	27
The Red of the Robin	28
Filling the Shelves — By Numbers!	29
Oh! For an Old-Fashioned Fairground!	30
An Ode to the Circus of Yesteryear!	31

*   *   *   *   *

For Christian Love — Always!	32
Moving Upward — Every Day!	34
To Be! — Loving Christians for God! And Trust!	35
Teach All Our Children — *The Ways of The Lord!*	36
To Share — With the Babes — Of the World!	37
Love The Lord God	38
Good Friday and Easter '95	39
My Prayer for Today	40

BLACKPOOL — 1994

There's been joyous celebrations, in Blackpool, Lancs, this year,
For double anniversaries, have come around to share.
The Tower has stood, a hundred years, an actual century,
And for a hundred and fifteen, *The Illuminations* have been seen.
This year, there was one more addition,
To Blackpool's, great *Pleasure Beach* fame.
And the world's, tallest and greatest, *Roller Coaster*
Has been launched, to boost, tourism trade.
Standing in forty-two acres, of mind-blowing rides and fun,
Are also, five other *Rollers*, (and ride on all those! if you come).
One, is the *Revolution*, where you loop-the-loop, — both ways!
Another, is Europe's *Grand National*, with the only, twin-track, known.
Six and a half million people, flock to this seaside, each year.
Many, to visit this *Fun Fair*, and to try the other rides here,
There's *The River Caves* to cruise through, *The Long Flume* is popular too!
And now there's even *Beaver Creek*, for the kiddies to join in, with you.
Alice in Wonderland also, is a ride for the young ones along,
And *The Greatest Show on Earth* with its razzmatazz, is also there to view.
But, when, you've enjoyed, rides and sideshows,
Then welcoming Blackpool awaits,
And the Shops, Cinemas, Shows and Stores, are there for your delight.
The Horse Drawn Carriages, Famous Trams, ply the *Golden Mile*,
Along whose length, stand three great *Piers*, for yet more merriment.
Please, don't forget *The Zoo Park*, the *Stanley Park* — (Donkeys too!),
And *Grundy's Art Gallery, Sea Life World* and the Pool in *Sandcastles* for you.
Yes! You are sure to love Blackpool, any year, that you come.
But, our Hols, in Blackpool, this year,
Has been a *Special* one.

AN ODE TO GRANDAD

Slowly, the door always opened, and quietly, shortly, was closed.
His footsteps, soon limped, up our passage, and his walking stick clicked on the ground.
Grandad, once more, was arriving, out of the cold and the rain.
Laughter, once more, soon abounded, and he beat me at Cards once again!
Whist was one of our pastimes, *Rummy*, and *Snap*, as well.
But, *Seven of Diamonds* was favourite,
And this game, I rarely played well.
Drive the Old Woman to Bed, was terrific!
We laughed, till we both nearly died.
And how I did love, my Dear Grandad,
The poorest, who made me, most glad.
Always, at close of each visit,
Worn hands, in deep pockets, he'd delve,
And always, from down in the corners,
A *Farthing*, with *Robin* he found.
Sometimes, a solitary *Thrupence*, into my hands he would slip,
Not to mention, some Pastilles, or a pen, from a seagull's quill.
Just time, for a last game of *Conkers*, which out from those pockets he picked.
Then fond farewells, till the next time, and out in the night he would slip.
This Man, entrenched in my memories,
Passed Over, when aged eighty-three.
And this year, with Caring Hubby, in tow, *His* Resting Place sought we and found.
From twelve, I am now nearly sixty, my *Grandad* is ever so near.
Yes! I wept when I laid those first flowers — With Joy!
For No One, was ever that Dear.

GIGGLES

Do you get *The Giggles*? I ask you Everyone?!
Can you Laugh, as we do, and join in, all the fun?
There's many a Joke, goes through our house,
Off the Stage, on TV, from the Press.
Do you Lap them all up, as we do?
And join in the jest with zest?! —
Till the tears, roll right down your faces?
We rock, and roll! nearly die!
Till we choke, and our heart races,
And our sides Ache! oh dear! Me-oh My!
Whatever next, will They tell us?
What more can They shake us with — Please?!
We need to draw breath, and wonder, sometimes,
But giggle, we must, or freeze!
'Cause it can make you hot, all this Laughin'!
If *Andy Capp* and *Flo* is about,
Or what of *The Perishers, Horace,* and All!
See *Griffin's Drawings*, and shout! —
What-a-Mercy! How maze They'm all Lookin'!
Are those people, really like That?!
All they wrinkles! they lines! and the blubber!
All they chins! above all that there fat!
I think, we were All, made to giggle,
And laugh our way, all through our lives,
And with Great Comics, here, as we have,
There's No problem, on that score, just laugh!
I'm not going, to start here, to name Them,
Those Comics, whose laughter, brings (or brought!) Cheer!
But with them around, there is always —
A giggle! a smile! and a Prayer!

— Pass the tissues — Quick! ha! ha! ha!

THE JOY OF A JOB

Up in the morning, early,
The Dawn Chorus over, they've flown!
Down to the kitchen, for Breakfast —
Lonely! — it's awful alone!
Nobody there, with a Greeting,
No one to cheer, no one smiles,
Never a chat, o'er a teacup,
And not a relation for miles — *But!*
Once you've caught bus, at the corner,
As soon, as you're one, of the throng,
And that promising job, is there waiting,
Then at last, you can feel, you belong.
What a joy, you can know, from employment,
— In Charge, of one Niche, all your own!
What a buzz, you can get, from achieving there,
— With the trust, and confidence shown, — *For!*
Whether, it's sweeping up leaves, folks,
Or whether, it's managing tills,
Whether it's Nursing, or Football — (aught else!)
— A Job! soon brings friendship — Pays Bills!

HOPES

People of pleasant persuasion,
Producing their product of Peace,
Portraits and *portents!* of pleasure,
People now pampered, per piece;
Populace, purposeful, Praising,
Precious each person to God,
Prayers and predictions by Prophets,
Pence, not from pensioners barred!
Pleasing presenting of presents,
Parcels from paradise brought
Plentiful, painless precision,
Parties and Pantomimes sought;
Placidly preaching for Jesus,
Pleasantly profiting prose,
Paintings and penmanship treasured,
Penalties past, and closed.
Just some proposals, improvements!
Policies perfectly planned,
What a dream, what a Play, what perception,
Could still be preparing for Man.
(Yippee!)

1994 — *D-DAY* AND *REMEMBRANCE* — 50 YEARS ON

Remembrance Day or *Poppy Day*, has come, and gone, once more.
Again, we *Honoured* and *Revered*, the Ones, who Fell, in War!
For our tomorrow, They Gave Their Today! How Great Their Sacrifice.
Young, Robust, and *Full of Life!* They Offered ALL for us.
This year, was truly Special, a Great Anniversary,
For 50 years, have slipped on by, since *Campaign Normandy*.
On June the 6th, in '44, Three Million Troops, at *Least*
Assembled, on our Southern Coasts, on France, to be released.
They formed, the Greatest *Invade* Force, The World has ever known,
And hitler's tyranny in France, was soon to lose its hold.
The Allies' Plans, well laid, in fact, from Spring of '43,
Were Ready! Awesome! to behold, to sail for Victory!
Churchill, Montgomery, Dwight Eisenhower,
Great Commanders from Commonwealth too!
United, combined, by sea, air, and land, This Mighty Force —
To free, on Europe — At Large! — Occupied!
Whole Countries — By Terror! — Sieged!
Not to mention, the plight of The Jews —
By Torture! — To Death Camps! — Seized!
Yes! it was *True*, and *Great* Men, who planned, through NEED! that Force.
And *D-day* finally happened, That Day, Grievous for *Thousands*, of course.
Over the Channel, They made Their way, Those Ships, and Boats, and Craft,
Filled with COURAGEOUS, HUMBLE, MEN, well versed with Their Treacherous Task.
To the meeting place — *Piccadilly Circus* first,
Out in the Channel, deep,
And then, across the rest of the Sea, to the Beaches of France, They did creep.
To Landings, on *Utah, Omaha, Gold,* — *Juno,* and *Sword,* as well,
How Great, the Mission of Every Man, to FREE, our World from Hell!
No! This *Remembrance Day*, This *Poppy Day* must NEVER be FORGOT.

Surpassed, in History, and World War II, for EVER, It will NOT!
Easy to say — *They will not grow old, as we who are left grow old!*
It's simple, to just be Grateful ONE Day, while still our lives, we hold.
At the going down of the SUN, and in the Morning we MUST
remember THEM.
Knowing! — For Certain! — That HEROES! — ALL!
(Even those who returned from the foe),
Are Guaranteed Life! — For Ever! — in Heaven!
And Love from us all, here below.

For *Freedom* They BOUGHT! for us All! — and LIFE!

BLOOD SPORTSMEN!

Fox Hunting, is barbaric,
Of that, there is no doubt,
And I'd ban it, from tomorrow,
If I had sufficient clout.

Stag Hunting, even more so!
Such use of *Stately* beast,
It's only *Sport?!* for Terrors,
And such folk I like the least.

Otter Hunting too — I cry!
For Mercy, for such life.
Who, sane, would dare rob streams, of Joy,
And think they have a case?

Badger Hunting too, is crass,
Of mindless ilk, to crave,
And Foxes, Stags, Otters, All!
Are due their time and space.

Culling might be needed,
All reasoned hearts, concede,
But Marksmen, as at *Pheasant Shoot*,
Is all that we would need.

Why should backward gentry,
From ages past hold sway?
And still spout *Mirthless!* pastimes,
Are just for them to pay?

Progress, means, we All advance,
And change They! surely must.
Red Coats, Ripping Dogs and all,
Cast to endless Dust.

Let these Monstrous Huntsmen,
Suffer for a spell,
While seeking, better ways, to spend
Their wealth, their time, their Hell!

Charities, could use their time,
Unfettered, are they not
By need, to *Chase*, by honest means,
To even fill their gut.

Can they not ride, Horseback,
O'er fence, and hedge, and field,
And feel they are still privileged,
A Horse to Own, and Shield? — FREE?!
(I pity them!)

IN SUPPORT OF TEDDY BEARS

Teddy Bears, are precious, Teddy Bears are pets.
Probably, everyone loves them,
If it's comfort you need, they're the Best!
They are cuddly, and soft, and wondrous,
Their fur you can brush, if you please,
They come in a good many colours too!
From dark browns, to yellows of cheese;
Their faces, are open, and honest,
Their glance, is so joyous — of fun!
The Aura, exuded's of pleasure,
A promise of something to come — (and they whisper —
    Soon you are going to feel better,
    Pick me up, and cuddle me — do!
    I'm waiting right here! — Come and Squeeze me!
    You'll love me for sure) — and that's True! — For!
Some people, collect them in hundreds!
All Shapes — All Sizes — All Sweet,
YOU! could purveyors of *Teddies* find,
They'd cater for you, such a *Treat!* —
Up on the Bed, you can place them,
One by one, on the pillow, they'll rest,
And all day long, like REAL TREASURES,
They'll sit there, and feather *your* nest,
Some, are bought dressed, and Elitest,
Some, have just one, mere, Bow-tie,
Some will *g*-rowl, if you press them,
And kiddies, love chances to try —
— To bring from their *depths* — these *Bear* noises,
(And mind you, some, only SQUEAK!)
But one thing, is patently Certain,
You'll too! be a Teddy Bear-*FREAK!*
'Cause once you get hooked on these Sweethearts,
Your heart, will be Softer, for LIFE!
But that spells, *Good News* really, don't it?!
So, why not buy TEDDY for Wife?!

TO ALL *WOULD-BE* VALENTINES — (1994)

Inspired by the thought of Valentine's Day drawing near — and how much more I love my beloved hubby now, 31 years after the Day we Wed (through thick and thin!) — UNITED, we were!

Valentine's Day! is upon us,
Feb 14th, is now drawing near,
I wonder, to whom, you'll be sending,
A Card and a Rose, of Cheer?
I wonder if you REALLY love them?
I wonder, if YOUR LOVE *will* last —
— All the Trials, the Pain, and the Upsets —
— We have to leave, in the Past?
So often, at first, Full of Passion!
And Certain our LOVED ONE's for LIFE!
We then, quite undaunted — Later —
— PART from, simply o'er strife,
Divorce *IS* horrid and shameful,
Joint children cared little for too!
So be SURE, when you write this year's Valentine Card —
— And the person you love — *IS* true!
That you don't later — *just up and leave them*,
OR, *stray*, along your life's way;
Be *Certain, DEVOTED, Be Faithful,*
And *DETERMINE*, to stay that way!

— *It's so worth it!*   X X X

ILFRACOMBE — OF THE 50s

Ilfracombe, is a beautiful place,
E'en the name, rolls right off the tongue!
It's brave, and strong, and exciting! —
— A Seaside, that basks in the Sun!
The Cliffs, and the Rocks, stoutly, stand there —
Absorbing, the might, of the Sea,
Mighty, does *Capstone Hill*, climb there, still —
— From the Prom, straight up, and it's Free! —
— To try, and stroll up, its pathway —
— Zigzagging, its way, to the top.
(Mind you, when breathless, you're getting —
— That, may be, the best time to stop!). — But!
The views, at its peak, are stupendous!
The rocked, beach, below, is unique! — Then
— Away, from this scenic — *Starter*, —
— Play *Putting*, pass the Theatre — then creep, —
Backward, along to the Harbour, (it bustles!) —
— And that way, there's yet one more beach.
— There's Gift Shops, and Cafés, a plenty, too!
And, the Ferry, glides in, from the deep,
The Harbour, is sheltered, so board Her! —
— Right out, in the Bay, she'll soon glide —
— To *Lundy Island*, she'll take you —
— Again, see the Views, far and wide — Then! —
When, you return — 'Combe, is waiting —
— Discover, at last, the Town, — For! —
— Once you've ascended, Streets, steep there —
— All that you seek, can be found.
The Main Street, is level — (Thank Goodness!),
The Locals, will greet you, as friends —
— You can't beat, a North Devonshire-Welcome!
— And the Service, you'll get, never ends.
There's the Cinema there, worth a visit — Then! —
— 'Round to the Seafront, you'll go.
Take in — The Parks, and the Flowerbeds,
Take Snapshots! buy Ice Creams!, See the Show!
— Have a wee bite, in a Café,
Write all your Postcards! take Stock! —
— That this is so pleasing, this place here,
And the walks, everywhere, are such fun!
Then note This down, in Your Diary!
That, next year, right back, you will come!

LOVE'S HOPES — FROM A WHEELCHAIR

Belovéd Love, How I love Thee!
— Standing there, so Fair.
What is it, you have, which Calls me?
— For truly, I want, to Care.
Your Perfume, here, is wafting — Close!
— Scenting, the warm Summer breeze.
Birds, high above you, are skimming —
— High to their nests, in the trees.
Nature's Hues, too!, are around you —
— Clear, in the flowers, at your feet.
No florets, in anyone's garden,
— Gave this faint heart, such a treat.
All those Pinks! and Reds! and Yellows!
All the Rainbows, shades, displayed.
Gleam out, from all around you —
— From Greens, as from Everglades.
Still, there is nothing, to match you.
— Were ever Eyes, so Blue?
Did Ever, Charm, from a Lady,
Swing me, as high, as you do?
Could I soon Call, to Court You?
Would you walk, at my side, with Me?
— Down, by the brook, to the Seaside?
Can I soon, talk, with You?
Often I've sat — watched you glowing —
And heard your laugh — ringing with Joy!
How often, out travelling, I'm Jealous —
— I've seen you, with t'shy *Butcher's Boy!*
Still! — hopefully soon, I *will*, run, to Greet You!
— There'll be smiles, and never a Care!
Our TRUE LOVE, shared, will Blossom!
— Once, I can leave, this wheelchair!

FOR THE SAKE, OF A CHIP!

I'm off to the Chippies'! — *said Alice*,
I fancy, a big bag, of Chips!
I'll scatter, the salt, all about *um* — Then! —
— I'll give *um*, a *Vinegar Fix!*
I'll come out the Shop, all delighted!
— I'll no doubt, burn, finger and thumb,
As I rush, to pick up, the first one! —
— 'Cause, I can't wait to get *um*, in *tum*.
No doubt, I will have, to breathe, on *um* — And! —
— Shake the bag too!, in a trice —
— Just so I eats *um*, more quickly — 'Cause! —
You can't beat a Chip!, they'm so Nice!
Right now! Right here! — I can smell them! —
— With Juices, in mouth, running Free! —
— You can keep, all your boiled, mashed, potato —
— Some Chips! I am buying! — For Me!
Into my mouth, I will pop them,
I'll give everyone, a big chew,
I'll slowly walk home, getting fuller!
— They'll be gone, time I get home, to you!
Why don't you come, along, with Me?
Your Company, really would please! — And! —
You could buy, yourself, Chips! Also! — And —
— I'd finish, your Cone off, — with Ease! —
Caw! Yeh! — that's a great idea — Stella! —
— Go get on your coat, quickly do!
And — If you decide, to Pay for us Both — Then! —
— I'd like me, some FISH!, with mine — too!

(Please!)
— *ha! ha! ha!*

PRAISE AND CARE FOR OUR ELDERLY AND VETERANS — ('95)

Alf, is a goodly Neighbour, of ours,
He's a Window Installer — Retired!
He's only *ONE!* Veteran, of World War II,
But it's time, His Story! — was shared.
For *Victory Day* — 50 years on — we remembered,
And *our* ALFRED, still clearly, recalls —
— The Day, "The Father" — saved him! —
— Plucked him, from Hell! — and Death's Jaws!

In World War II — Alf was a Sailor,
To France, with his Ship, he did creep;
Hundreds of men, were aboard *Her* — And!
— Most of them — Feared! — *The Big Sleep!*
Close, into shore, his Ship, anchored —
— Shells! — Falling 'round! — Rained-in!
Great numbers, of Vessels, were gathered there —
— What Explosions! — What Hell! — What a Din!

Flames! — fired from shore! — were a'leaping!
— Guns Boomed! — Ships Blazed! — *Good Men Died!*
Alf, though, was called to the Captain —
— Was told, to move Ships — nearly cried!
Soon! — he boarded the small boat — (with belongings!)
Was rowed, to his New Ship, nearby — *Then!*
— On board, he turned, to see — his *old mates!* —
— There'd been little time, — for *Goodbyes!*

Right Then! — one great Shell — flew on over!
It burst — in his Old Ship's — sides!
And Poor Alf, just stood there — in Horror!
— In a Daze! — He saw friends! *Drown and Die!*
For slowly, his first Ship, slid under the Waves —
— After tilting, one end, to the Skies!

What a Nightmare! to Live with! — a Lifetime!
— Just ONE MAN, from War Years, so vile!
And Yes! That War Won, England was Victor! *But!*
For Veterans, and Old! — *Someone's Lied!* —
— For Evils, they *now*, have to still, suffer here!
— Who Cares? — Where's the Thanks? — When's the Prize?

BURNT TOAST!

What's that there Smell?! — I'm here Smellin'?!
And look at that Smeech! comin' through —
— Right into, the Lounge, from the Kitchen!
The Smoke, — swirlin' 'round, — is quite Blue —
— And Grey! — and Black! — and Revolting! — And! —
I know, what you've done, and that's True! —
'Cause that! — was supposed, to be *Toast* — Dear —
— You've done it, *Again!* — haven't you?!
First, you place Bread, on the Grill Pan —
— Then you go, and find somethin', To Do! —
Well! — you can *Forget it* — my Sweetheart!
— I'm not eatin' — *Burnt Ash!* — for you. — So! —
Please! — put away, all that Butter —
— (Or Marg, that I know, you Prefer) — And! —
I'll do my own *Toastin'* — Darlin' —
— When I can breathe again — yer!
Caw! — look at the flames — in that Cooker! —
— This time! — you've really excelled — And! —
— Out there — a little while back Pet!
— We thought — we heard somebody — yell! —
Just get out the Aerosol, Sweetheart!
— Then, spray it thick! — quick! — all about!
And keep, all the *Crumpets* — belovéd —
— (The *Tea Cakes* — you'd burn, too! — No Doubt!)
Yes! — when my Mates, come, in-a-minute,
— *Us!* — is goin' to sit, in the Shed! —
'Cause, you can't See-for-Lookin' — in 'ere, Dear!
— And you'd turn, all embarrassed, and red —
No! — We can't go and rest, in the Garage — And! —
— (I know, it's much bigger — by Far!)
But! — Right now, I better Confess, Love!
— There's a worse *Smog* — out there — from the Car!

NON-SENCE! — AT *THE SALES*

I went, to the Sales, — last tomorrow.
I put, my worst foot — to the rear.
I went down, the Lift — to the top floor.
All the shoppers, piled in, at least four.
I pushed past six women, behind me,
All rushing, to slowly reverse.
If they'd only stopped — to go faster,
They wouldn't, have ended up first!

They picked-down, their gloves, they kept finding.
They tried-off, two hats, at a time.
Their purses, were burstin' with space, folks!
Their Cash Cards, they Lost — Ten-a-Time —
Each one, they used, for One item,
Non-plussed, The Store, made a Gain,
And, soon, all the customers — vanished —
Up! to the basement's Fame!

The Bargains, up there, were terrific!
The Prices put up, all fell down!
So cheap there, the Goods, were revalued!
The Moths, in your purse, flew to town!
Handbags, were sold, by the foot, there.
Jumpers — unleaping just lied — So!
Loaded! — I went out the entrance. *And!*
Rejoicing! — on t' bus, I just cried!

(Oh dear! dear!)

A LITTLE "HOPE" FILLED PLEASURE

Perhaps, you enjoy, a wee Challenge —
— In Puzzles, For Prizes, you vie.
At Bingo, The Jackpot, could fall in your lap!
Or, This Week, "The Pools", may come up, me ole chap!
— Even, the "Spot-the-Ball", you could site,
And *"Hope"*, buys the tickets, in Raffles, and might —
— Win you, a Holiday Cruise, in the Sun,
Or a Flight, somewhere, over the Moon!
And Certainly *"Hope"* springs Eternal, down here —
Happily promising — *"Fun"*, and Good Cheer!
(Even the 'Penny Falls', at the Fair — Or! —
— Down on the seafront, and out on the Pier!).

E'en my own, Dear War I, War Torn, Father,
— Backed! — on Horse Races, each week! —
He bet pence! on Lester Piggott — (of '35) —
While still a mere 'prentice — (but fleet!),
And before Him, on Sir Gordon Richards —
My Dad, would back, '3d each way!' —
Along with his mates, at the Factory — (For Fun!)
— In *Faith* and *Hope*, many a day.
Often! — with Winnings! our Family, lived well!
— For my Father, could never earn more —
— Than £5, from t' Factory — For Ever! — *Or!*
His War Pension, would Cease! and for Sure!
Yes! — We five, in His Family, saw t' Benefit! —
— Self-Righteous! we never once, were, But,
Three times, each Sunday, and Three times each Week!
— *He!* and my Mother — (God Bless Them!) —
Made Certain, Our Saviour, We'd Seek.

Money! like Blood, is a Resource, to Tap!
— To Harness, For Life! every Day!
Our "Father", knows, who'll *Best* Use it —
— The Humble! —
On Dear Ones! Some Needs! and Fair Play!
Charity Benefits — Sometimes! —
— Hopefully, often, a Lot! — *And!*
Remember, you Winners, with *Love*, (if you please!)
— A Kindness! *Un*shared! Will Not!

SORT OUT PRIORITIES — FIRST!

Marriage should be *vowed* — to Last-a-Lifetime!
Marriage — *In Love* — *IS* Great!
Marriage Vows — ARE — *till death us do Part!*
No Partner, should Ever — *Want-Out!*
Sex, before *Marriage*, just Weakens, the Bond — For! —
— If only to Bed! — you can go! Then!
— Something, Solid, is Lacking! —
— Together! — in Trust! — *First* Grow!
Bed, is for Fools! — Not, the *Be-All* — For! —
— If you Want, your Partner — for Life! —
— Other Contingencies — *First!* — matter more!
If Bed, is *ALL* — You'll have strife. — So! —
Build *first*, on all your joint interests — AT LARGE!
Enjoy *First!* — Your Hobbies! — Joint Sports!
Find out, requirements, can *All*, be agreed! — And! —
— Visit, your families — Rejoice!
Promise to Loved Ones — *Devotion!* — That! —
— You'll grow, more together, Each Day!
Promise, to keep, that Promise — *FOR LIFE!* — For! —
— The journey, could be — A Long Way!
Marriage IS — one great Adventure —
— A *Patchwork Quilt* — of *Design!* — And! —
— Through, *thick and thin*, you *MUST HONOUR!* —
— *First* Passions — you quickly — Define! — So! —
Visit *First* — Theatre! Cinema! — Church! —
Enjoy some Meals Out! — Talk for Real!
Potter around! — share your Laughter! — and Save! —
— Go for long walks — and Reveal — *FIRST!* —
— How you both feel, about *CHILDREN* — Their Rights!
THEN: Joyously Following Wedding —
— A Lifetime — of *Honeymoon Nights!*

UNITED — THE WHOLE JOURNEY THROUGH!

Till death us do Part? — Our Marriage is!
That, is for Certain! — We Know!
I'll always Love Him! — He'll always Love Me!
Through Laughter! and Pain! — we just Grow!
From the Start — we made the Decision — That! —
— Together! — For Sure! — We Would Stay! —
Each to the Other — *Vowed it* —
Determined, we were — To Sow! —
— Into our Marriage — *Devotion* — And! —
Trust! and Faithfulness! too!
Why?! — Should one, stray, to Another? —
— No Human — is Perfect for you! For! —
No Mortal, was born, to Perfection!
Some Days! — I'm worst Wife — in the Book!
NO! — He brought my Life! *Marriage*, and *Meaning* — So! —
Why?! — should I Seek Out! — or Look! — For —
— Some Stranger! to take, and *Dismantle!* —
— *ALL* — that my *Man's*, given Me?
Yes! — He gave me, Our Children! — Our Home! — and His Pay!
PLUS: — A Life's Book — of *Love's Memory* — *NO!* —
I know, which side — *my bread is buttered*,
— From, this Nest — to Fire! — I'll ne'er jump!
And *Frying Pan* — just don't come in it —
For *Green Patch* — o'er Fence! — I'll ne'er Look!
Fidelity — breeds — understanding! *And!*
Birth Signs — will indicate too!
Why Hubby, will sometimes, take stances, he does —
— Or say, sometimes, Cruel things, to you! —
You just have to WANT — To CARE! ALWAYS! —
In His Arms — You *Can* Stay! Your Life Through!

It's so worth it! Ha! Ha! XXX.
(again!)

SOME LIMERICKS OF FUN!

There was a young man, of Dundee,
Ate Fruit Cake, and Jam, for his tea —
The Waitress, he sued,
For being quite rude,
But, in Court, she sat, on his knee!

There was a young lady, in Cork,
Who picked up her knife, and fork,
And ate, roast and peas,
Forgot, to say, *please*,
And was thrown out, to walk home, to York!

There was a large dog, in the night,
Who gave this old lady, a fright,
She cried, till the dawn,
While his howls, just went on,
And she moved, to get out, of its sight!

There was a small bird, in the yard,
The Locals!, just thought him, a card!
He'd peck up their crumbs,
While they even, banged drums,
And the Cats, and the Dogs, sat on guard!

There was a sweet rose, in the sun,
And gladly, she bloomed, for the fun!
But then, it did rain,
She thought it, a pain,
And wished, to the Shed, she could run!

There was, a leek pie, on the sill,
Who wouldn't cool down, but still —
It shone, in the sun,
And smiled at yeast bun,
And, soon, folk indoors, had their fill!

There was, a small stone, out of reach,
Who wished, it was set, in a peach,
The ebb tide, came in,
It mustered, a grin,
And the sea, swept it, way up the beach!

FOOTBALL!

Are you a Football Supporter?
Do you follow, the Matches, each week? —
From the start, to the end, of the Season? —
— Are you a footballing — Freak!?
Perhaps, you prefer, *hands-on* Rugby?
(*All* Football, presents, such a feast!)
Is there one Team, you shout loudly for? — and —
— (No doubt, there's a Club, you like, least!)
Do you holler, those Rhymes, so gladly?
Do you clap, and applaud, all t' game through?
Do you stamp your both feet, in the stands there?
Do you rise, as one man, *when t' goal's due?*
At every Home match, are you present?
In all weathers! — (unless you have flu?)
Perhaps, for your Team, you'll journey Away! —
Proudly wearing Their Emblem, on you —
— On jerkin, or sweater, rosette and scarf, —
— (Some, *highlight*, their faces, now, too!) —
How, super, it is, just to be there! —
— From the time, the singing is due, — that is —
Once the Teams, all prepared, and trained highly,
Have jogged onto field — (mascot too!) —
You can let down your hair, get delighted — And!
— Tell Linesmen, and Ref, what to do!
It's just great then, to be breathing!
The exhilaration, you get, is grand!
No wonder, it's the World's greatest Sport here!
And it's played, in 190 — Lands!
And was Founded in 1863 you know,
What a time to span, so supreme!
What a tradition, for a Player, to follow,
So many played like a dream!
From Matthews — the Charltons — (and Pelé!)
The roll of such names, journeys on, — and
All those true Sportsmen, you Honour,
Every time you join in the throng — (e'en these days!)
— *Isn't Rush, just the greatest*, they tell you! — and! —
Seaman! — my! — what he can do! — Yes!
Every Match, is so different, so special,
So you won't miss many, will you?!
(And who knows, with you there a'chanting away —
To Wembley, your Team! — could soon Go!) — *TRUE!*

AN ODE TO THE CLOWNS!

How jolly, are our Clowns here!
How full of Life! and Fun!
What joy! they bring, along the way,
We love them, every One.
Before they even — *Start their Show!*
Before — *It's* — *On-the-Road!*
They take, a long time, just to *Dress!*
And first, their *Face!* they'll unfold,
They sit, in front, of t' mirror —
— With choice of *make-up*, all 'round,
And nearby, never far away —
— Their *Wig!* is surely found.
Patiently, with steady hands, the razzmatazz, begins —
And they *paint*, and *highlight* — all their face —
(With Skill!) — So we can't ignore, their grins!
Around their mouth, they'll colour white — Then! —
— Bright Red, 'round the edge — with Care! —
And, from ear to ear, the smile, will stretch,
(Any pain! — they'll hide! — right there!)
Their eyes — they'll *paint* around, as well!
And — *Soulful* — Comic Clowns! —
— Add tears! right down their visage, —
— But laughter! — still resounds!
They make the most, of their noses too! — And!
— Some, add spheres, of red! (or black!),
While others, *paint*, red triangles — on —
— so a Comical Face, they won't lack.
Some Mark Crosses, on eyes, or on cheekbones,
And some, draw, *big lips*, turning down!
But — however, they alter their Faces —
— The end result — *IS* — *The Clown!* —

So, when at a Party, or Circus, or Fête,
You enjoy, all their antics — great Jokes!
Or see, all the tumbling!, or magic! — and mirth!
Remember, as well, won't you folks! —
The time they gave you, before t' Act, began,
And to the end of the Show, from the Start!
Just relax, and delight, in the pleasure they share!
And the Good! — they All do! — From the Heart!

THE RED OF THE ROBIN

The Robin, is a *cheery* bird,
It's so friendly, and chirrups!, all day,
In Winter, especially, it's noticed,
And its *red breast*, just gives it away.
Hidden, from gardeners, it never will be,
As it bobs, along, on the fence —
— Its *red patch* — so bright! — and so glowing!
— It's so tame, and — patient!, — has sense!
The Sick, and the Elderly, Love them! —
— I know, I have seen their display
And the Dear Elderly Lady, I once knew here —
— Could Time! — When they'd Call! — Every Day!
Perhaps you should know, their past history,
Perhaps, you would then, love them, more! —
For, one of them Loved! — our Dear Saviour! —
— The Day, — *HE!* — was Hung! — and for sure, —
This brown, feathered morsel, of Caring!
— Swooped down, to cross member, of CROSS —
— He didn't believe, he was seeing —
— *Perfect Man* — Dying! — of course!
He noted, the blood, slowly dripping —
— From around — OUR LORD's Crown! — of cruel thorns!
Down — *Pure Love's* Face, it was trickling —
— Perhaps — small birds too! — grow forlorn! —
For! — this little bundle of MERCY! —
— Flew nearer, our Saviour — *Hung High* — And! —
Attempted! — to tweak Hell's *halo* of Nails —
— Off t' *Noble Head*, — to the Skies! —
But! — one of those wicked thorns, Pierced him!
— The blood, flowed, from t' little bird, too!
And since then, that spot's — been *Bright Crimson*,
— Again, God's Love's, proven, — for You!

FILLING THE SHELVES — BY NUMBERS!

One thousand Loaves, just arrived here! — And! —
Twenty-three boxes of Ham!
Six Crates of Milk, need the Fridge — Dear! —
And there's, sixty-four, parcels, of Jam!
There's thirty-two choices, of Fats! — Come!
From Oils, Marg and Butter, to Lard,
And ninety-two, Cans of Potatoes, —
And Peas and Carrots, fill t' yard!
There's Tins of Fruit too! by the Dozen!
And of Fresh Cream! there's cases of 'Leven.
Then there's Custards and Rice, to be stacked, here!
At last count, I marked, seventy-seven.
Ten packets, of Flour, have just burst! here!
Two members, of Staff, are now white!
And, with broken Eggs! Raisins! and Currants!
We'll bake us, eight cakes, by tonight!
Ten hands, of Bananas, are coming,
And Fourteen pounds, of Spring Greens;
You won't see us here — soon! — For-Lookin'.
The speed, we go, has to be seen!
At, twenty-four miles, to the hour, folks!
We *shelf-loaders*, chase round this Store!
Avoiding, the eighty-four Shoppers.
'Tis, a wonder, we're here, any more!
Still! — Soon 6 o'clock will be ticken'!
All day, I'm watching, the clock!
Just guess, who'll be first out the doorway,
The Stock, can then, sit here — and Rot!

(Oh Dear! again!)
(I've seen too many Will Hay Movies!)

OH! FOR AN OLD-FASHIONED FAIRGROUND!

Bring back the "Fairgrounds", of yesteryear too!
The ones, *All!* the Family, enjoyed,
For the toddlers, right up to the Grannies,
(For some risks! they too! — "FUN" employed).

Why? — did the "Noah's Ark!" — cease, to exist?
Who? — thought "Roll-a-Penny" defunct? (Now 2ps).
Where? — was the "Moon Rocket" dumped? — (Out in Space?!).
How? — did the "Coconut Shy", get replaced?
— There still! Could be "Boxing Booths" too! (For the Males!),
— *Well!?* — Couldn't there? — (and "Swing-Boats!" please!).
And! What? — of the "Straws"? and the "Corks"? and the "Ducks"?!
— With a Prize! every time, to seize?
When? — will the "Cards", for the "Darts", return?
And those "Rings", thrown round Gifts there, to Win?!
— "Hoop-La" they called it (*And* Bingo Stalls too!),
— Us Old Folks! Like Fun-at-the-Fair, Same as You!

AN ODE TO THE CIRCUS OF YESTERYEAR!

Once, there was this Giant Circus, arrived —
— To a grassy, great field, outside town.
The "Great Top", was soon, up in place there, so high!
— The "Centre Ring" beckoned us all, passing by —
— Wond'rin', if *"We"*, could get there (or try!)
— When "Box Office" opened, what tickets, to buy!
And the whole Site, was bustling, the noises rang clear,
And so many Animals, filled us with *Cheer!*
There were Lions, and Tigers, and Elephants — great!
Horses, and Doggies, and Doves, —
Budgies, and Llamas, and Zebras, and Seals!
Kangaroos, Giraffes, Camels, and Mules, (and *More!*).

These days, Sad Folks! STOP Enjoyment!
'Cause — Jugglers, Acrobats, e'en Clowns,
And High Flyers, Athletes, and Tumblers *alone,*
Don't! attract us, the same, out of Town.
With a Change! and some Cash, in our pockets once more,
— What Fun! again soon, there could be,
For! — "Do-Gooders", and Pundits of Caution — (and *GLOOM!*)
— STOP Pleasure! and ALL JOLLITY! — 'Cause —
Some Animals too! — Love a Challenge!
For Carers, of Mirth! — they'll Show-off!
Why? should their Talents, be wasted?
(Cruel Masters! are Nil — Opera Toff!?).

Jeremy Beadle's Show, proves it!
"You've Been Framed", is so great! on TV,
Some Clever Stars! — of all species!
Love Performing! for "You", and for Me!
NOT! Silenced! Ignored! or made Jobless!
(We've ALL, had enough — of all that), — *And!* —
Along with the laughter! the Pop Corn! the Claps!
— The Candy Floss! Hot Dogs! and Ring Master's Chats!
The Circus! Could! once more, glorious be.
With Fond Trainers — *Those Gifted!* once more
— Could we see.

(Yes! and the so-called "Do Gooders" live on and talk to Vegetables probably as well! poor dears!). (And think little of Divorcing and *Abandoning* their own children *Cruelly,* too! many of them!). BAH!

---

*   *   *   *   *

FOR CHRISTIAN LOVE — ALWAYS!

It's great to be a Christian, with CHRISTMAS, very near.
No other Season's like it, any time, all year.
Good Friday, and then Easter, teaches *Life o'er Death!*
And if we seek Repentance, Sins — Forgiven, behind are left.
At Whitsuntide, *The Holy Ghost*, on Chosen few, Descended,
And ten days, first, before That act, to Heaven, our Lord, Ascended.
The message, left us Sinners, though, was ne'er to feel, alone,
And at Harvest Time, we Praise His Name, for ALL, that He has Given.
How can one *doubt* THE BIBLE?! — *Ignore* The Gospel's Store?!
If only Man, would LISTEN! We'd journey, safe! and sure!
No other Creed, is like it, NO GREATER LOVE, is found,
Than when you Follow Jesus, the Joy, will just Resound!
For Ever he is near me — *I know! — I have NO doubt!*
Through Trial and Tribulation, MY GOD, is ALL! — About!
His Spirit — *IS* — within me, I need Him, till I die,
HIS WILL BE DONE from all my heart, from roof tops — I would cry! —
Have mercy, on the Poor Ones, the Sick, the Blind, the Lame,
No Wealth, you'll take to Heaven — Please?! — Start to PLAY-the-GAME!
On Earth, there Is, sufficient, for All, to live, their Span —
To share, we were intended, our Lot, is for, ALL MAN!
We do ALL, need to Worship, at Mary's BABY's Crib.
Shepherds, even WISEmen, knelt, Their Gifts to Give!
— I was born, in better times, into a Christian Home,
The War, soon overtook us, but Wholesome GOOD, was found —
In Every corner, of this Land, at Work, *at School, at Play,*
And it was After, that Great War, we *LEFT THE NARROW WAY.*
Three times, every Sunday, and Three times during week,
Loving, *CARING*, Adults, made SURE, — MY LORD — I'd seek.
Then, one night, straight from Harringay — (on link!)
A Great Man, called my Soul!
Dr Billy Graham, spoke, and CHRIST, was REAL! — my GOAL!
I wish, I could Evangelise, from Pulpit, Hall, — for CARE!
I'd tell the world, that *My God Reigns* Advise them to Beware!
I'd be a *Light*, for Jesus, each and every day,
Here I am, send me Lord! is all I'd need to say.
At least, though, here near Christmas, I plead, you *all*, draw near.
To HEAR, My LORD, Call you! as well, No more your Sins to Fear!

Sing! some Hymns, by Isaac Watts, Charles Wesley, Tate, Heber —
They ALL, are GREAT! (As Others Are!) For you to Sing for Ever!
Buy the SANKEY Hymn Book — Pray! — At Table, and Night and Morn
With Diary of GOOD John Baillie, and Read, THE HOLY Word.
It's ne'er too Late, to Follow! The righteous, he ne'er came to Seek,
Only the Sinners, he sought for, so KNEEL, beg Forgiveness, and REAP!
What JOY, This Christmas, is waiting, to shower on us *all* from Above,
Approach HIS THRONE, Why don't You?!
Touch the Hem, of His Robe, and *Love!*
Yes! Send out your Cards, and your Presents,
(And accept a few too! — no doubt!)
Enjoy this GREAT Celebration! and place all your gifts, round about —
— Under the Yule Tree, so splendid,
The one you Adorned, with Care;
Package, the Gifts, for the Children,
And Cook, All, the Christmas Fayre.
Just enjoy, every day, every Party
(Yes and enjoy a few drinks — if you Can!)
Just PRAY though — Please?! — and Remember, THIS BABE, became PERFECT MAN!
— Our Lord, Our King, FOR EVER! from this — Nativity.
Then Change! For Good to Enter,
More Wholesome, Again! We Can Be!

(Praise The Lord God Remember HIS! Favoured Command! and Sing the Carols ALL! — Hallelujah!).

MOVING UPWARD — EVERY DAY!

The Lord, IS — my Shepherd!
Is He Yours? — Too?
Do you Sin, very often? — For! —
— I do, and Mark You! —
— Each Day, with remorse, I've to ask Him —
— To Forgive, — All the Sins, — I Confess — And! —
I *know*, that He Does! — Always!
And quickly, He stoops down, to Bless!
He's Just There! — Waiting! — to Listen! —
— To every Woe, every Prayer!
What a Friend! — How He Soothes! — How He Pardons!
— Without Him to Guide — What is there!
My Life — would be worthless — Confusion!
— My Rock, He IS!, and that's True!
And Reader! — if troubled, and worried —
— He'd give you, this Freedom, too! — For!
— Sinners!, alone, He Died For —
— At Golgotha, on Calvary's Tree!
And the Righteous, He ne'er came to seek — Dear!
He sought out, weak folks, like me! — So! —
— That includes *YOU! — Too!* — don't it?! —
— Mere Mortals, mistakes, always make — And! —
We foul up each Day! — somehow!
— No matter, what Care, we take —
To be Watchful, and Faithful, and Loving
— It's easy to try, hard to do! — BUT!
— *HE KNOWS!* — God Sent Him — to Love us!
Please kneel, and address Him! — Yes! You!

(Sursum Corda!) — To God Sometimes!

TO BE! — LOVING CHRISTIANS FOR GOD! AND TRUST!

Open your heart, to Jesus,
Give, your Saviour, a Chance!
Trust in God, also, *The Father*,
Give *Abba — The WORD* — a glance!
HIS WISDOM — IS — past understanding,
Why should He!, discuss plans!, with You?
You could Not, Life! or Worlds! CREATE! —
— Or even less, know what to do!
YES! — HE! — gave us Birth, and FREEDOM!
— What do you do, with Your! Time?!
Do you most wisely — Use it?!
Do you Ever — try Hard! — to Climb?! —
Towards, your Heaven, — awaiting!
(Perhaps HELL, — You! CREATE! — and Prefer?!)
Decisions, You make! — with HIS FREEDOM —
With LOVE! — HE TRUSTS! — We'll soon, Learn! — For! —
— Christmas, devised He! for Sinners!
On Good Friday — HIS SON! — Died for Us!
At Easter — The Promise of Life! — is ours!
Do you Care? — at All? — or THIRST?!
No, words, can express, how I Love Him!
— You think *The Bible* — MERE WORDS?!
You think, with *Degrees*, and 'A' Levels —
HIS MIGHT! — is nonsense?! — For Birds?!
Do you merely believe — *THIS WONDERFUL WORLD!* —
— Scientifically started?! — with *Bangs?!*
How pitiful! — scathing! — and sightless! —
Humble man — Listens! and Learns! — and Then!
Reads Corinthians I — Thirteen, and begins to Trust and Love!

(For we are All Sinners here!)

TEACH ALL OUR CHILDREN — *THE WAYS OF THE LORD!*

More precious, than teachings, this HAPGOOD — would preach!
— This bishop! from *God Knows Where!* —
Are the TEACHINGS — of Our LORD JESUS — And! —
— You'll find *THEM!* — in 4 Gospels — CLEAR!

This bishop — OUR LORD — *FROM!* — Our Children — would *KEEP!*
— And declares! — He is Right! — from height high! —
He claims — Assemblies — at School — From *NOW ON!* —
— Are *Not! Needed!* — a MERE WASTE OF TIME!

There are too! some headteachers — now here!
— Agreeing — *BLASPHEMING'S* — *CORRECT!!* —
How far, from Hallowed! and *NARROW WAY!*
— These dignitaries *All!* — have crept!

No Wonder — The *GREEDY!* AND *PERVERTS!*
— Are massing — in *SIN!* — EVERYWHERE!
No Wonder — with mortals, like these to Guide —
— *Glue,* and *Drugs,* — become Children's Fare!

I was taught — by Very — *Disciples-of-God!* —
— Of Truth! — From Assemblies *TRUE!* —
Their *ADULT!* Lips — Taught us — *HIS WILL* — And
— The Joys of *HIS* HEAVEN — we soon *KNEW!*

I would strongly Advise — those with Learning! —
— With 'A' Levels, or Hard-earned *Degrees!* —
To Assimilate — *ALSO!* — *GOD'S WARNINGS!* — (BELIEVE!)
— Then *FIRST!* — *STRIVE!* — *HIS LOVE* — to APPEASE.

Teach, *ALL OUR YOUNG* — The Commandments — *TEN!*
— Teach them — *BEATITUDES* — Too! — *AND!* —
Jesus Said — *SUFFER THE CHILDREN* — *TO ME!* —
For the sake — *OF GOD'S WRATH!* — See You Do!

(And Amen to that!)

TO SHARE — WITH THE BABES — OF THE WORLD!

God — always Blesses — the Children,
He bids them, to Jesu's knee!
He *Listens!* — to *All* — they are saying — (or singing!)
When Dancing! — He Stoops — Them! to See.
But! U.N.I.C.E.F. surely, will tell you —
— The Hell! and the Shame! They Unfold! —
While Starving, in 3rd World Countries! (e'en these days!)
Or Dying! — of Thirst! — or from Cold!
Oxfam — too!, will soon tell you —
— The Disease! and the PAIN! — *BABES*, are pressed —
To Suffer! — and Sicken! — and Die for! — *And!* —
In some lands, they are sorely Oppressed!
Charity, FREEDOM, and *Loving!* —
— Should Always! — be poured! — on the young —
We owe it — as Jesu's Disciples —
To Show Them! — We care! — Make Them Strong!
So! — When, in good health, with your youngsters, —
You Pass! — in the Street, *Saints of Gold* —
— Holding out Charities' Boxes —
Try to spare Coins — And! — Unfold —
From your Hearts, as well as your pockets —
A PRAYER! — For these Sweethearts — so Poor! — *AND!* —
PRAY — for the Greedy — amongst us now! — *That!* —
— They Pay themselves *LESS! — GIVE OUT MORE!*
Wickedness! — truly Abounds here!
Babies — are *Here!* — *Born,* for *CARE!* —
(Money, in Banks! — Counts for Nothing! —
— So Please! Teach them quickly, — *TO SHARE!*)

LOVE THE LORD GOD

Love the Lord, with all your heart!
Never be Unkind!
Let your Love, touch everyone,
And you will surely find,
That God, will shower, you, with Gifts!
And, stoop down low, to Bless! —
— You, and all your People.
You'll find, True Happiness!
For Life, was meant for Sharing!
All, He Gives, to you!
Time! and Fun! and Money!
Stay Longer, shared by Two! — OR!
— Three! or Ten! or Fifty!
Like Fish and Loaves — for Few!
Miracles do, still happen!
He'll Feed! a Host! through You!
Or Heal, their Pain and Sorrow,
— Help Scientists — succeed!
For God, loves those — Who help Themselves! — And!
— First! — *Care!* — for other's Need!
He's waiting for your Praises,
— And Thanks! for this Glad World!
It's not His fault, it's Dark here,
We've not used FREEDOMS, Well!
BROAD WAYS — ALL! are Craving!
Perversion, and Sins! pile High!
Just like, one big, manure heap!
And Lust, defames, the Sky!
So! Why don't you kneel, right this minute,
All Sinners, are full of Remorse,
It was, for us all, Jesus Died there,
Just share in God's Love, from the Cross!

GOOD FRIDAY AND EASTER '95

No Wonder, we call Friday — *Good* — on April 14th this year,
And indulge, a time to remember,
How PERFECT MAN, so dear,
Gave All He was, a sacrifice,
For Sinners' Souls to FREE! — And —
Forgiveness He bled, and earned, for us all, —
— At Golgotha, on Calvary's Tree,
And if we dare to kneel, and Pray,
And Repent, Seek, Knock, and Ask,
Jesus Christ our loved Saviour,
Will still stoop, to His Wondrous Task —
— Of releasing us all from our sinnings —
— So plentiful now, they can be,
But washed in His Blood for Ever,
Wholesome, once more, we can be.
This is the promise from Heaven,
If you'll read, The Gospels, — Find Out!
Only the BIBLE, can help us,
Planks, or motes, from eyes, He'll throw out!
Then onward and upward, Rejoicing!
Each day fulfilled, by Release,
From *Evil and Greed!* to *Love and Joy!*
From Death, to Life, He'll lead —
— All of us pitiful Sinners,
(But the Righteous He ne'er came to Call!)
So remember, all this, and *Good Friday*
Will be one of the *Best Days!* of all — But!
Following on from *Good Friday*
Three Days later on April 17th,
We'll, all of us, celebrate EASTER! again,
And Chocolate Eggs, we will eat.
For this day is even Greater,
Our Lord rose to Life, once more, and —
The message, for all mere mortals — *IS!*
Life's VICTORY, achieved, Evermore!
Through glass now, we only glean darkly,
The LOVE our GOD, Did provide,
But with Easter, we ALL, can be Certain,
Our futures, need not, be denied.

Amen! and Hallelujah!

MY PRAYER FOR TODAY

Dear Lord, once more, I approach You,
Once more, I need, to confess.
Once more, I need also, to praise Thee,
And thank Thee, for life's happiness.
For beauties, of nature, around us,
For bird song, and flowers, and trees,
For mountains, and hedgerows, and rivers,
With fish there, streaming — to please.
For all of the walks we can take Lord,
Uplifting our hearts, as we go —
With loved ones along, who we cherish,
And all these I bring — them, you know!
There's Mother and Father and ---------?
And aunties and uncles belong,
Not to mention, grandparents,
And cousins, and friends here along.
Thank You! For peace, Lord, and pleasure!
Thank You! Each step of the way, and
Please bless the poor, and the weak, Lord
The homeless, impoverished — show! —
All of the unemployed Jesus,
The sick, and the shattered, the old!
The children, the blind, and retarded — just!
How beautiful, they are, to know!
Bless all Evangelists Jesus,
A billion souls, Morris Cerullo, would save!
How great, His mission, of *Life* Lord,
Please, grant, all he wishes, below!
For me, I would love Thee, for ever,
To *Abba*, and Heaven, let me grow!
(And that means Both of us here — *Father*!)
                                          Amen.